Jack Jowett lives  Fylde Coast. He is Navigator with the founder member Fylde Mountaineeri  and for many years walking tours for Ramblers' Holidays in the mountains of Northern Italy and Scotland. In addition he has served as a Voluntary Warden of the Lake District, providing Mountaineering Instruction for young people training for The Duke of Edinburgh Award and outdoor activity schemes for young offenders.

THE LANCASHIRE-LAKELAND LINK

by
JACK JOWETT

with photographs and maps by the author

OWL
BOOKS

First published April 1994
Owl Books,
P.O. Box 60,
Wigan WN1 2QB

ISBN 1 873888 60 0

Designed and produced by
Coveropen Ltd., Wigan. Tel: (0942) 821831
Printed and bound in Great Britain

CONTENTS

This book is dedicated to my wife, Dorothy who has accompanied me on all the walks and has helped in the preparation of the manuscript.

FOREWORD

'The Lancashire-Lakeland Link' is a book that will bring pleasure to all those interested in Lancashire's countryside.

At a time when there is increasing awareness of the importance of our local environment, it will bring knowledge and pleasure to a wide variety of people. There is something here to delight the historian, the geologist, the naturalist and the ornithologist as well as the rambler.

The reader will be taken along pleasant country paths, through beautiful unspoiled scenery and will have drawn to their attention everything of historic or natural interest on the way.

Lancashire County Council supports those wishing to enjoy the pleasures of the countryside. I am particularly pleased that we have recently marked and signposted many of the footpaths described in this excellent publication!

Cllr. Louise J. Ellman
Leader of the County Council

INTRODUCTION

Experts seldom agree, but one thing that all medical advisors do concur upon is that exercise, and especially walking, is beneficial even essential for good health for all age groups. This is especially the case for retired people who often have the time to enjoy pleasures which perhaps in earlier life eluded them.

Furthermore, walking can be made much more rewarding if it is combined with other interests, such as bird-watching, photography, sketching, visiting places rich in history or abundant with flowers and trees. In doing so, we escape from the noise and pollution of urban life and find that our walks not only bring us physical benefits, but also psychological relaxation whilst exploring unspoiled countryside where motorists never intrude.

It matters not what time, distance or height is achieved. Many mountaineers, like myself, finding that they can no longer be 'tigers', may now find that attaining the summit of a thousand feet can bring as much satisfaction as the 'epics' of yesteryear. As one famous climber said, "It is being there which counts".

This book suggests routes from central Lancashire to The Lake District, which provide plenty of alternatives for the walker. No expensive gear is needed. Most important is a pair of comfortable boots or shoes. It is not necessary to wear heavy footgear. There are plenty of lightweight boots on the market. A light rucksack is needed containing a waterproof, spare jersey, food and, in addition to this book, the appropriate maps. **The Ordnance Survey 1:50,000 _Landranger_ maps indicate all the rights of way. Numbers 102 and 97 cover the area. The _Pathfinder_ maps (2.5 inches to 1 mile) are clearer and give more detail but, as they only cover a small area, many more maps are needed.**

For most of the way, the route is obvious and well sign-posted so that detailed instructions are not necessary, provided a suitable map is used. There ae plenty of variations and alternatives available, so that the walker may plan his way, taking into account his physical capability and the weather.

This is a walk which may be done at any time of the year. Indeed it is arguable that late autumn, winter and early spring are the best times, when there is snow on the hills and the distant views of the mountains assume alpine splendour, when the beech leaves are bronzed in the autumnal glow, or when the first snowdrops peep among the woodlands. In addition, bird watchers will have chance to walk through one of the richest areas of bird life in the country, and those whose interests lie in seeking rare and wonderful flowers or butterflies will delight in the abundance and variety of species.

The route passes through an area full of contrast, ranging from canal towpaths, disused rail tracks, riverside, parkland and elevated moorland.

Time should also be allowed to visit castles, pele towers, and stately mansions along the way.

It is an easy walk which may be done in sections, to suit the capability of the individual walker and may be facilitated by the use of two cars, one at either end of the days walk, and we are never very far from pubs, cafes and public transport.

In cold conditions, extra precautions are needed, especially for older folk. A good waterproof should always be carried and extra woollen clothing. The most common omission, however, is the protection of the lower half of the body. Thermal underwear, especially 'Long Johns' are recommended and there is now a good selection of lightweight garments available. For those who are 'getting a bit thin on top', a woolly hat prevents much bodily heat loss.

The route finishes on Orrest Head above Windermere, a modest hilltop, but one of the finest viewpoints of the Lake District.

THE LANCASHIRE TO LAKELAND LINK

Preston to Bilsborrow

12 miles

WE start at the Ashton Basin. This is on Aqueduct Street, behind 'The Lime Kiln' pub. There the southern end of the canal terminates and there is a small park.

In a short time we are clear of the houses and into the pleasant Fylde countryside, with the Bowland hills ahead with Parlick and Fairsnape most dominant. The canal meanders in a westerly direction, behind Salwick Nuclear Power Plant where there is a cutting lined with overhanging trees which makes pleasant walking, especially in springtime.

Every bridge over the canal has a number on it and at **Bridge 26** there is an attractive pub with a somewhat un-attractive name 'The Hand and Dagger' where bar meals are served. Now, the canal takes a curve to assume a northerly direction, passing about a mile east of Kirkham, then going underneath the M55 motorway at Bridge 28a.

From **Bridges 29** to **32**, the route goes east, then turns once again north-east before heading northwards again. This change of direction is sometimes confusing. It was designed in order to link with a proposed route to the coast at Fleetwood but the project was never started. The meanderings, however, give changes of views and the masts of the Naval Communication Centre at HMS Inskip are always prominent.

At **Bridge 32** there is a canalside pub, 'The Bay Horse', alongside 'The Jolly Roger' family boat centre, which pro-vides teas and refreshments. Two miles further on we

PRESTON TO BILSBORROW   12 MILES

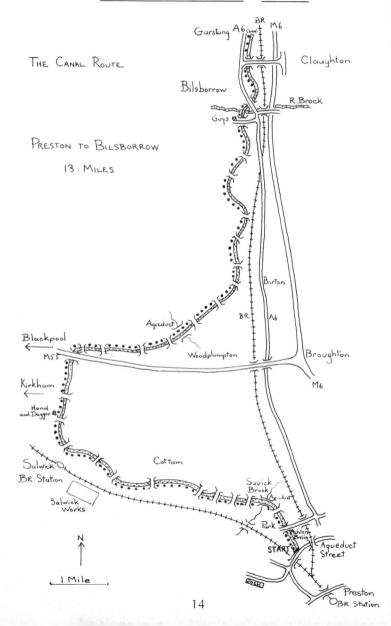

THE CANAL ROUTE

PRESTON TO BILSBORROW

13 MILES

Garstang A6 Canal BR M6

Claughton

Bilsborrow

R. Brock

Guys

Barton

BR. A6

Broughton

Aqueduct

M6

Blackpool

M55

Woodplumpton

Kirkham

Hand and Dagger

Salwick Br. Station

Cottam

Savick Brook

Aqueduct

Salwick Works

Park

Ashton Basin

Aqueduct Street

START

N

1 Mile

Dock

Preston Br. Station

14

come to **Bilsborrow**, where there are three pubs, a cafe and shops.

Situated alongside the canal at **Bridge 44** is 'Guys'. This is a recently constructed development consisting of attractive thatched buildings which incorporates 'Owd Nell's Tavern' with canalside tables. The adjoining bridge is one of the very few which have been widened.

I have a special reason for my regreting the disappearance of the old humped-backed bridge, for it was here, many years ago, that one frosty March morning, a memorable incident occurred.

Cycling with my friend, we were heading for the Bleasdale Fells when a young lad came running towards us shouting that his two pals had fallen into the canal. They had been sliding on the ice and, when attempting to go

The Roebuck Inn at Bilsborrow.

Brock Valley

underneath the bridge, the ice gave way and they fell through. One had managed to scramble out and run for help. Another was near enough to the edge for us to be able to reach him and drag him out, but all we could see of the third was the top of his cap. There was no sign of life.

"You'll have to go in and get him", shouted my companion (I was never quite sure why I was chosen!). Forgetting that I was wearing my nailed boots, I jumped in. It was deep and cold and it seemed a long way to the bank where my friend awaited to drag us onto the towpath.

The poor lad looked dead but I tried some artificial respiration and after much water had emerged from him, he began to show signs of life. "What do we do now?" was the next question. We decided to put the lads on our crossbars and cycled to the nearest pub. I will never forget the reply I received when the door finally opened — "Sorry, we're closed"!

Desperately, we tried the next pub and, by this time, news had reached the village that something exciting was happening and as this is unusual in Bilsborrow, a small crowd of people had gathered, headed by the vicar. The landlord, probably sensing that he was the centre of some sort of drama, was quick to tend to our needs. Hot drinks, blankets and a warm fire soon worked wonders and we were soon fit enough to make our way back home. The vicar then came with a pile of dry clothes and we were none the worse for our adventure.

When I reached home, my sister could not understand why I had left home that morning attired in shorts and climbing boots, only to return dressed as a vicar!

Continuing our walk, we soon arrive at the Brock Aqueduct, where the river had to be lowered and a weir constructed in order to engineer the river crossing. The Brock is a pleasant little river which rises among the Bowland Fells quite close to us. There is a fine riverside walk which continues as far as the tiny hamlet of **Bleasdale**, in the heart of the Bowland Fells. The wooded slopes of Beacon Fell may be seen, where a small country park has been made. This gives great pleasure to thousands of people who visit it every year, yet, in spite of its popularity, still, at non-holiday periods, may give a variety of quiet walks through moor and woodland.

The River Calder Aqueduct is now crossed. The Calder, like the Brock, rises in Bowland but, unfortunately, there is no continuous right of way along its bank.

The village of **Calder Vale** lies in a hollow a few miles to the east. Here there is still a very active cotton mill. In bygone times there were dozens of small mills, situated close to fast flowing streams which gave them water power, but the few remaining ones are powered by electricity.

On our right are the parklands of Claughton, the residence of the Fitzherbert-Brockholes family, whose emblem of a Badger decorates two of the nearby bridges. ('Brock' is the old country name for a badger.)

As we approach **Garstang**, the canal turns westwards before crossing the River Wyre by a single span aqueduct and we soon arrive at the Garstang canal basin situated on the fringe of this pleasant market town.

'Th'owd Tythebarn' is situated on the canal side at Garstang. In contrast to some of the old buildings, the Tithebarn is older than the canal itself. Meals are served on long trestle tables and in winter huge logs blaze in the biggest fireplace I have ever seen. The building also houses a canal museum. Nearby there is a Marina and caravan park. From here, it is only a short walk into the town where there is plenty to see.

Garstang is on the side of the River Wyre and there is a pleasant walk along the bank, starting from the municipal centre and car park. From here also, a diversion to our walk may be done. This is described on page 24. Across the fields, on the far bank of the river, we can see the ruins of Greenhalgh Castle on a small hillock.

Greenhalgh Castle

"A Horse, a horse, my kingdom for a horse"

These immortal words by Shakespeare were supposedly uttered by Richard III of York in the height of the Battle of Bosworth Field in 1485 when his magnificent white charger was slain and he cried for help which never came. Instead, Lord Stanley, who had sufficient men and armour to win him the day, stood by, waiting to see which way the battle was turning and in the heart of the fray, he changed sides. He joined forces with Henry Tudor of Lancaster, so that Richard's army was defeated. Then, as it is recounted in the play, Stanley placed the crown of England upon Henry's head. Thus Henry Tudor became Henry VII and, by his marriage to Elizabeth of York, the houses of York and Lancaster became united. Stanley was rewarded by being made Lord Derby and granted vast lands in the North of England. Naturally, by his acts, he made many enemies and so, to protect his lands, he was given a licence to build defences; among these, was Greenhalgh Castle near Garstang.

This explains the reason why so many pubs, parks and roads in Lancashire bear the name of Stanley or Derby.

There is also a legend that one of Lord Stanley's forbears, Sir Thomas Lathom, who fathered many illegitimate children, had a son he particularly liked and so, wishing him to be his heir, he placed the babe under a tree where an eagle had built a nest. Taking his wife there, he tried to persuade her to adopt the baby as their son. However the plan failed and the estates were handed down to his daughter.

So, that is the story which gives rise to the numerous pubs called "Eagle and child" and why this emblem is incorporated in the crest of the Stanley family.

Greenhalgh Castle was not built for residence. It was a military fortress, erected upon a small hillock to the east of Garstang. It commands an extensive view of the countryside and, later, when a bridge was built over the River Wyre, a watchtower was placed so that a sentry there could keep an eye on traffic along the roads and swiftly send a warning to the castle in times of danger.

There were four towers connected by turreted walls about sixty feet high. So it was virtually impregnable.

A moat surrounded the castle and the entrance

was by means of a drawbridge which gave access to the Southern tower.

The castle guarded the lands around Garstang until the civil wars when Lord Derby supported King Charles I against the Roundheads of Oliver Cromwell who laid seige on the castle in 1644. They were unable to take it, and finally it surrendered.

The castle was totally destroyed by Cromwell's men, apart from the Western tower which now still stands amidst ruins.

There is another strange legend concerning a member of the Cromwell force besieging Greenhalgh Castle; he was Peter Broughton. The story goes on to say how, one evening, he paused upon Gubberford Bridge near Garstang to gaze down at the river Wyre when a lady dressed in white appeared. It was his errant wife who had, in the meanwhile, bigamously married a Cavalier officer. Apparently, she was not even capable of being faithful to him and whilst Broughton and his wife were apparently becoming reconciled, the Cavalier appeared and stabbed to death the unfortunate lady. Then, the two men realising that she was indeed a faithless woman, buried her by the banks of the river.

Now, it is said that the ghost of the faithless wife appears of an August evening, dressed in white.

So that is the story of Greenhalgh Castle. There is not a lot to see, but it is a pleasant walk, starting near to St. Mary's Catholic church, then along Castle Lane, to the castle. The path continues beyond the castle and it is possible to walk along pathways into The Forest of Bowland area.

Garstang

GARSTANG has always been a thriving market town where produce from the rich Fylde farmlands could be sold, but in former days transport was the main problem. The huge Shire horses pulled their carts along the muddy lanes which connected the scattered villages and farms until the canal came along, connecting the town to Lancaster, Preston and thence to South Lancashire. The Thursday Market Day was an important day when horses, cattle, cloth and all manner of other goods were bought and sold in the Market Place, by the old cross. This stands in the centre of the town, outside The Royal Oak, which was an important coach staging post.

Then came the railways. The station was built on the main Preston to Lancaster line just outside the town and bore the name, 'Garstang and Catterall Station'. The Kenlis Arms stands near to the site, which was also the junction for The Pilling and Knott End Line.

The advent of motor traffic closed the canal for commercial use but all motor transport between Preston and Lancaster went through the centre of the town until, in the 1920s, the A6 road bypassed it. Then later, the M6 was constructed but this also provided no convenient access to Garstang.

Perhaps Garstang owes much of its present day charm to the fact that it is now by-passed. The cross and market place are still there and market day is still held every Thursday. The canal is now, in summertime, busy with pleasure craft of all types.

Good car parking and shops, alongside a modern Leisure Centre and schools have made Garstang an attractive residential area and a focal point for residents living in adjoining country villages.

A Diversion into The Forest of Bowland — 6 miles

THE path starts at the main car park on the north side of Garstang, close to the River Wyre. A pathway follows the western bank from where Greenhalgh Castle can be seen upon a small hillock.

On our left are the sports fields and ahead is the embankment which once carried the Pilling Pig Railway over the river and on to the former Garstang and Catterall Station. This embankment is now used as a water catchment from the river. Water is extracted from the River Lune and conveyed underground to Abbeystead, where it flows into the Wyre, flowing down to here before passing by pipeline to the Franklaw water purifying plant near Churchtown.

It was at Abbeystead that an accident happened several years ago when residents from the nearby village of St Michael's became victims of an explosion whilst inspecting the underground installations. Several people were killed and many sustained terrible burn injuries. The cause of the disaster was attributed to the presence of methane gas in the system, but it was difficult to prove this fact. Ironically, the object of the trip to Abbeystead was to convince the people of St Michael's that the diversion of the water from the Lune to the Wyre would in no way increase the danger of flooding at St Michael's, an area which has always been subject to disasters caused by the river bursting its banks during times of heavy rainfall.

On a summer's day the river at Garstang is a happy place where children paddle, cricketers play, people walk

Parlick from Beacon Fell

with their dogs or we walk along on our way towards the Bowland Fells which we can see ahead.

Continuing along the river bank for half a mile, the ford is reached where a footbridge takes us over the river and by following the quiet lanes in an easterly direction, the main railway and the A6 motorway are crossed by bridges, after which we come to the little church at **Barnacre** set amid the trees. Nearly at the top of the hill is the entrance to Barnacre Lodge Estate, surrounded by woodland. Here there is a path which climbs parallel to Parkhead Brook, then bends north to Birks Farm and then to Burns Farm, which provides excellent farmhouse meals.

Now, bearing north-west, we descend to Grizedale, more commonly known as 'Nicky Nook'. This is a popular walk with local ramblers and it is indeed like a bit of Cumbria in Lancashire. The name 'Grizedale' is of Norse origin and means the valley where pigs were kept. Nearby Bleasdale is also a Norse name, meaning the dark valley.

Every time I climb the hill at Nicky Nook I remember when, as a small boy, I was taken there by my teacher. Once a year, she would organise a school outing to Nicky Nook. This was long before the cult of Outdoor Pursuits had been invented. We would travel to Fleetwood on the tram, then over the ferry to Knott End where the 'Pilling Pig' would convey us to Garstang. Then over the fields we walked to Nicky Nook. This was my first glimpse of a high mountain. For me, it was Everest and from that moment, mountains became part of my life.

Winter scene from the Forest of Bowland.

Following the delightful valley north-east, the old reservoir is reached. Remains of old rail tracks and small quarries used in its construction are seen by the path. There are two larger and more recently constructed reservoirs higher up and out of sight from the valley, which we soon leave and climb a steep path amid the bracken to gain the trig point at the top of the hill. From here, there are splendid views in all directions, especially to the east when in August, the purple heather is in bloom. There are not many paths there, for the area is preserved mainly for grouse shooting. There is one magnificent route, however, called The Langden Track, which goes from Bleasdale to The Trough of Bowland.

Our way goes in the opposite direction, down to the pretty village of **Scorton**, which is notable for the fact

Nicky Nook in winter.

that there are no pubs there; just one cafe. The nearest pubs are on the A6 road, so it is there that we are heading!

From Scorton, the Trough road climbs a little hill, passing some grey council houses on the right. Shortly after, there is a footpath sign which points towards the River Wyre where there are several large gravel pits which were excavated during the construction of the motorway. These are on The Duchy of Lancaster Estate which is owned by the Queen. Now they are being converted into a pleasant lakeside parkland with amenities for fishing, birdwatching or just walking and enjoying the peaceful setting. A pathway through the area goes to Street Bridge but our best way is to bear left along pleasant lanes, past Cleveleys Mill and to the 'New Holly' on the A6 road. Carefully crossing the busy road to gain the minor road on the far side, we are soon at the bridge where the canal route is joined.

Garstang to Galgate

8 miles

IF the diversion through Bowland is not taken, the alternative is to follow the canal which, after leaving Garstang, meanders first north-west, then north-east, passing over the site of the former Knott End railway. We now enter one of the finest sections of the canal; to the west, the flat farmlands stretch to the sea. The area is sparsely populated but every few miles there is a hamlet with its church, village school and pub. Each is a self-contained community. They have names such as **Nateby, Winmarleigh, Forton, Cabus** and **Cockerham.** Eastwards, the land rises towards the Forest of Bowland. The long line of heather covered moorland forms the skyline. There lie the Bowland villages: **Scorton, Dolphinholme, Abbeystead** and **Barnacre.** There also are the rich estates belonging to the Duchy of Lancaster and the Duke of Westminster, whilst lesser estates are at Bleasdale, Littledale and Quernmore. Most of this land is barred to walkers because of its use for grouse shooting but recently, the Lancashire County Council have successfully negotiated access agreements over certain areas and it is hoped that there will be more sections open to walkers in the future. In the relatively few areas where access is permitted, there is no evidence of abuse by those who wish to roam these lonely hills. Walkers respect the right of the landowners to close the hills at grouse shooting time and in times of drought, when there may be risk of fire. A voluntary warden service patrols the area and tries

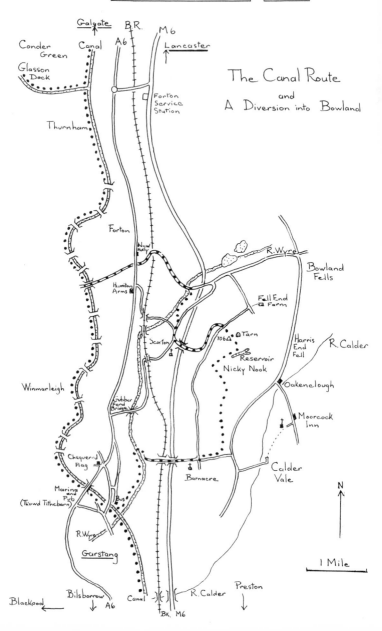

GARSTANG TO GALGATE 8 MILES

Galgate

Conder Green

Glasson Dock

Thurnham

Canal

A6

B.R.

M6

Lancaster

Forton Service Station

The Canal Route

and

A Diversion into Bowland

Forton

New Holly

Hamilton Arms

Scorton

Gubber Ford Bridge

Winmarleigh

Chequered Flag

Marina and Pub
(Th'owd Tithebarn)

Bus

R. Wyre

Garstang

R. Wyre

Bowland Fells

Fell End Farm

706△ Tarn

Reservoir

Nicky Nook

Harris End Fell

R. Calder

Oakenclough

Moorcock Inn

Burnacre

Calder Vale

N

1 Mile

Blackpool

Bilsborrow

A6

Canal

B.R. M6

R. Calder

Preston

The canal near Glasson.

to ensure that there is always a good relationship between owners and walkers.

Continuing our way northwards along the towpath, we enter one of the best stretches of water. There is an abundance of birdlife. Herons are often seen, much to the consternation of those who have outside fish ponds. Sometimes one may catch a glimpse of the elusive kingfisher, whilst swans, mallards and coots are common. In late springtime they sail proudly along with their little convoy of chicks. In summer, all types of butterflies flit among the bramble hedges bordering the path.

To the west lie the parklands of Thurnham Hall as we draw near to **Galgate** where there is a Marina. Also, it is the junction of the branch line of the canal which descends through seven locks in order to reach sea level at Glasson Dock.

Galgate To Lancaster

8 Miles

AT Galgate, there are roadside pubs, a marina, a cafe and the buildings which once housed one of the oldest silk mills in the country. It was formerly a corn mill, powered by the River Conder.

It is at Galgate that the canal section to Glasson Dock was opened in 1826 giving access to the canal from the sea. In addition, a railway from Glasson into Lancaster meant that ocean going vessels could have ease of access to both the canal and the main railway line to Preston. This enterprise put paid to Sunderland Point as a dock just as the opening of Preston docks in 1892 greatly reduced the use of Glasson, causing the railway to become extinct and the line now forms the pathway of the Lune Estuary Walk which will be following into Lancaster.

Glasson Dock, however, is still used as a port and goods are conveyed to their destination by road.

About a mile along the towpath, we are able to see Thurnham Hall among the trees on the far side of the canal. It is now not open to the public but, a few years ago it was possible to be guided round the Hall by an electronic cavalier who, by means of a recording system, would explain the history of the Hall.

This has always been a strong Catholic area and the Hall was owned by the Dalton family who have given their names to Lancaster's square. Their burial place was at the Chapter House of Cockersands Abbey situated on

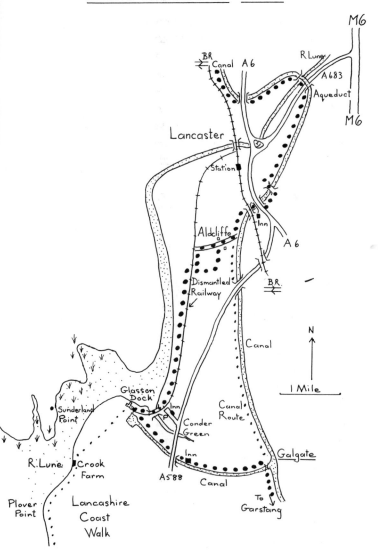

33

Glasson Dock. At this lock, the canal descends to sea level.

the coastline about four miles away. There is not much left of the Abbey, but there is a legend that there was a tunnel from there to Thurnham Hall. This is now generally disputed, yet I remember a farm lad a Cockersands showing me the entrance to this underground passage and furthermore, he said that he had been in it for some considerable way until it became blocked. There undoubtedly was a tunnel, but it is now assumed that it was for drainage. Another interesting fact is that, a few years ago a secret priest's hiding hole was discovered in the Hall and it is well known that in the days of the Reformation, when Catholic priests were ruthlessly hunted and often burnt at the stake, these hiding places were constructed for concealment or escape.

Halfway along the route to Glasson, we come to the former Thurnham Mill which has now been converted into a pub and retaurant, then as we walk along the quiet waterside, we can see an abundance of bird life including swans

Condor Green. This was the first stop on the former Glasson Dock to Lancaster railway line. It is now on the Lune Estuary Walk.

The canal near Condor Green.

which nest there and, in springtime their convoy of little cygnets are escorted by their proud parents. At Glasson Basin lie some elegant ocean going yachts and a few less elegant barges which have usually been decorated with traditional designs and are rented for leisure usage.

After The Basin, the final lock gate leads into the Docks where small cargoe vessels are berthed.

Behind the bus stop is the start of The Estuary walk which we can now follow into Lancaster, with The Lune on our left and the canal on the right, until the old iron railway bridge crosses the River Conder near to Conder Green where the attractive Stork Inn is situated.

Nearby is a Car Park, toilets and information centre from where we may read the history of the railway.

The path which continues along the old railway line, is a couple of hundred yards west of the pub and passes to the rear of Ashton Hall, the former seat of the wealthy industrialist and benefactor, Lord Ashton. It is now a golf club with an adjoining garden centre.

The path alternates pleasantly from enbankments to cuttings, lined by overhanging shrubs and bushes.

The distance from Conder Green to Aldcliffe is 3 miles and it is there that we join a leafy road past some luxurious houses to join the canal on the southern outskirts of Lancaster. Before reaching Aldcliffe there is a path towards the canal. This however is not easy to find. For the only time on the Canal Walk, we cross the waterway and follow it on the right hand side for a few hundred yards into the centre of Lancaster. Here, just before reaching the busy A6 road through the city, we arrive at 'The Water Witch' pub which used to be the canal stables.

Lancaster

Before continuing along our way, we must not forget that we are close to perhaps the most historic city in Lancashire, so why not pay a visit to St. George's Quay where there is an excellent Maritime Museum. Every year a festival is held there when the life and customs of old Lancashire are revived. This is the heart of the oldest part of the city, centred around the Quay, the Castle and the Priory. Here we can trace the foundations of the City's history which was built upon trade and industry. The Castle is built on the site of a Roman fort. Now there is very little evidence of Roman occupation, apart from the ruin of the bath house which is between the castle and the river.

On the hill in the centre of Lancaster stands The Abbey and the Castle, the major part of which is a prison. Parts of the Castle are open to the public when the Assizes are not in session. Dominating the grim entrance to the Castle is the life-size figure of John O'Gaunt although, in fact, he was only in the place for nine days.

It was at Lancaster Castle in 1612 that the trial of the so-called Lancashire witches took place. It is difficult to decide what is fact and what is fiction and no modern Court of Law would convict them on the evidence of a precocious young girl who readily gave information which sent members of her own family to the gallows.

Certain facts are undoubtedly true; that King James ordered that all convicted witches should be executed and witch hunters scoured the land in order to carry out his commands. For some time there had been certain

Character at the Lancaster Maritime Week. He is playing a type of bag-pipe.

families in the Pendle area of Lancashire who practised the Black Arts and, by means of clay models, were supposed to inflict ailments into people by pricking them with pins. Any misfortunes that local people suffered were attributed to their curses. The witches were often half-witted, disfigured or deformed and lived in extreme poverty, existing by begging.

The exception was Alice Nutter, a gentlewoman from a good family who lived at Rough Lea in Pendle Forest. She was implicated in the trial but refused to give any evidence in her defence. So, she and six others were found guilty, sentenced to death by hanging - which took place on the moor to the east of the city on the following day. A descendant of the Nutter family settled in Cleveleys on the Fylde Coast in the early twentieth century and gave land for the building of the church there. The streets adjoining their bungalow are called Nutter Road and Rough Lea Road.

The River Lune, or Lon, as it was formerly named, was an obvious choice for a port and was so used for many centuries, in spite of the problems presented to larger vessels caused by silting. This necessitated using Sunderland Point then, later, Glasson and Heysham but eventually the expansion of Preston and Liverpool made Lancaster's trade decline until it is now only used by small craft.

Nevertheless, in the eighteenth century, a thriving maritime trade developed mainly with the West Indies. Sugar, tobacco, wood, rum and raw cotton were imported and it is easy to imagine the aromas which filled the air in this busy quayside as the boats were unloaded.

Later, these same vessels would be laden with manufactured goods, such as floor covering, furniture and processed cotton bound for the West. Fortunes were made. In particular, Lord Ashton of the Williamson family became one of the richest men in the world, building his wealth on the production of huge textile and linoleum industries. He bequeathed money for building the city's finest monuments, including the Town Hall, the Queen Victoria monument, the Ashton Memorial and the completion of Williamson Park, which was formally a quarry. This provided sandstone for the city's finest buildings. The Park is crowned by the Ashton Memorial, which is a landmark for miles around and from its balcony, on a clear day, there are magnificent views. On a summer eve-

Lancaster Aqueduct, where the canal crosses the River Lune.

ning, this is the setting where there is music, dancing and plays by Shakespeare, performed in a woodland park.

So, instead of following the rather uninteresting section of the Estuary to the Aqueduct, why not walk through Old Lancaster? Wander into the little alleyways, like 'Bashful Alley', past the 'old satanic mills' to the canal side where brightly coloured passenger barges would, if you had time to spare, take you on a cruise along the waterways, accompanied by a most informative description of the canal and its history.

Lancaster to Warton

9 miles

AT Lancaster, we pass over one of the most spectacular features of our walk, The Lune Aqueduct.

As we leave the industrial area of Lancaster, the water becomes noticeably clearer and the scene is enhanced by beautiful gardens tended by houseowners who obviously love the waterside and often have their own little rowing boats anchored there. On our left, at **Hest Bank**, we can see the sea and it is from here that the old coach route crossed the treacherous sands of the Bay, often guided home by a light in the window, shining from the village inn.

Bolton-le-Sands is a pretty village, the old part being bypassed by the A6 road. The Packet Boat Inn may be conveniently reached by crossing the bridge. This, as its name implies, was a stopping place for the Kendal to Preston Packet Boat. At **Carnforth,** there is a children's play area at the point where our routes again divide. We have the choice of either walking through Carnforth towards the limestone hills of Warton and Silverdale or continuing along the canal to Kendal.

The Canal Pathway into Kendal

At **Capernwray**, the River Keer is crossed by another aqueduct, after which we pass under the railway bridge on our way to **Borwick** where, on the opposite side, can be seen The Hall which was formerly a defensive pele tower.

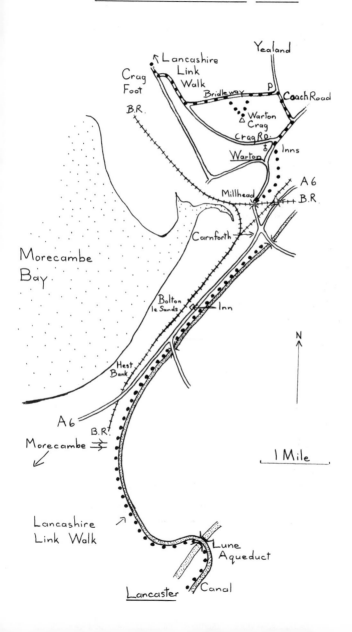

Canoeing on the canal at Carnforth.

The canal north of Carnforth.

Tewitfield marks the termination of the navigable part of the canal. Here, there are moorings, a camp and caravan site, picnic area and a handy nearby pub.

The canal ceased to be navigable in 1968 when the M6 motorway was built. Indeed, although the next section is very beautiful, its tranquillity is somewhat spoiled by the roar of speeding traffic on the motorway on our left, which crosses to the opposite side as we approach the village of **Burton.**

As **Kendal** is approached, the canal water's depth diminishes. Water is replaced by mud and water plants until, after the Hincaster Tunnel, the only hint of the canal is the occasional familiar bridge standing amidst the fields, unused and useless, just a reminder of the times when busy barges passed underneath bound for Kendal or Lan-

Locks at Tewitfield, 4 miles north of Carnforth.

Miniature railway at Steamtown, Carnforth.

caster. The waterway is now lost amid the Kendal houses, as is the old Roman Fort which once stood on a loop of the River Kent.

The route from Carnforth to Brigsteer over the Limestone Hills

At Carnforth, railway enthusiasts will be sure to visit 'Steamtown' in order to have a nostalgic glimpse into the bygone age of steam. There is a reproduction of the renowned, 'Thomas the Tank Engine', rides on a 15" gauge miniature railway and, at certain times, the opportunity to travel by steam to main line destinations. From Carnforth, we can cut across fields to the village of **Warton**. Now we are in limestone country and remain so for the remainder of the walk as far as Kendal.

Warton Village

JUST over a mile north of Carnforth lies the quiet village of Warton. Much of its tranquillity is due to the fact that it has been bypassed, first by the Romans, who ignored the fact that there was a Brigante fort situated on the summit of the limestone crag which overlooks the village, then by the Vikings. There are remains of these latter invaders at nearby Heysham and also at Heversham, but nothing at Warton and in recent years, the A6 clearway and the motorway both ignore the village. It is just outside the Lake District maps and very few signposts point towards the place. Indeed, there seems no special reason for going there at all. From a distance, the crag does not seem interesting enough to warrant a visit. Mostly, it is covered by trees and dense undergrowth, whilst the ghastly scar of a limestone quarry mars the southern face. (This has recently been made into a car park.)

Then why, on Independence Day, do the Stars and Stripes of America fly from the church flagstaff? The answer is that the ancestors of George Washington lived here in the seventeenth century, originating from the wealthy family of Kitsons of Warton Hall. This flag was specially flown from America, donated by a Senator and, moreover, had previously flown from the Capitol Building in Washington. Inside the church is the family tree of the Washingtons, also that of the Churchills who, through the Spencers, are also descendants of the Kitson family. And if further proof of importance was needed, there is, on the inside wall of the Tower, the coat of arms of Washington with three stars and two stripes.

In a secluded corner of the village, opposite the church, is the ruined Old Rectory which, along with several other buildings in Warton, is scheduled as of historical and architectural interest. Looking north-east, five miles away, we can see the limestone escarpment of Hutton Roof. Below lies the pleasant village of Priest Hutton. Here, in the sixteenth century, was born Matthew Hutton, a boy of humble origin but of outstanding ability, who became Archbishop of York and founded the school at Warton.

So, it is quite rewarding to spend a little time wandering round the village and if further inducement is needed, there are two excellent pubs!

Warton Crag

DURING the Ice Age, the glaciers carved out what is now the Lune Valley. This separates the gritstone and sandstone to the south from the northern limestone.

Now it is well known that this beautiful white rock will dissolve in rain water (by a chemical action), thus causing the caves, pot-holes and underground water courses associated with limestone and, although there are no caves of any speleological interest here, there are many unique features. If, again, we look towards Hutton Roof, we can see a fine example of a dip, or syncline, in the rock strata. On Warton Crag there is a dip in the strata towards Silverdale and it is believed that the water which issues from the rock at the picturesque Woodwell, actually comes from Warton Crag, four miles away.

There is a small cavern on the north-west side of the hill, known as Dog Hole. This has no significance to anyone interested in cave exploration, but has yielded some archeological finds which prove that it was inhabited by prehistoric men.

The Brigante Fort near to the summit is marked on the map but is difficult to find, being surrounded by dense woodland.

On the summit is a trig point and a recently reconstructed beacon, to remind us that this was one of the chain of beacons throughout the land which was lit at times of great importance, or danger such as the approach of the Spanish Armada in Elizabethan days.

Warton Crag is now a conservation area, bordered on

Warton Crag

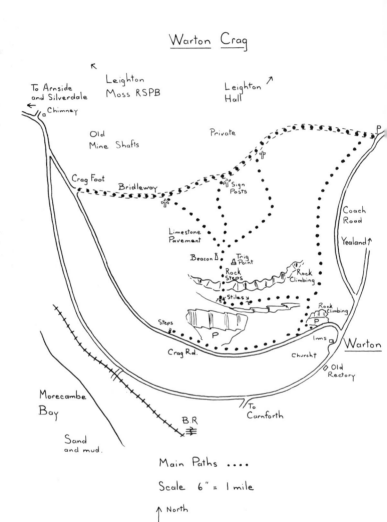

To Arnside and Silverdale

Leighton Moss RSPB

Leighton Hall

Chimney

Old Mine Shafts

Private

Crag Foot   Bridleway

Sign Posts

Coach Road

Yealand

Limestone Pavement

Beacon   Trig Point

Rock Steps   Rock Climbing

Stiles

Rock Climbing

Steps

Crag Rd.

Warton

Inns

Church

Old Rectory

Morecambe Bay

To Carnforth

Sand and mud.

B R

Main Paths ....

Scale 6" = 1 mile

↑ North

Clints and Grikes or 'Limestone pavement' on Warton Crag.

the north by the Bridle Path which runs east to west. There are access points at either end of this and the paths to the top are now well marked by wooden signposts. Routes starting from this Bridleway provide the easiest ways to the summit. They pass through fine woodland with a variety of trees, both conifer and deciduous, which provide a habitat for wild life, including deer.

On open sunny slopes, in June, wild orchids, primroses and rare rock plants grow, whilst in the woodlands are the flowers and fungi which thrive in pleasant shady areas.

The south side of the hill is more open and is lined by rocky escarpments which provide pleasant scrambles and also some rock climbing.

We are now at the halfway point of the walk and from the summit of The Crag, we can see the entire route, from Bowland in the south to the mountains of Lakeland in the north. Beyond the northern Bridleway lies the land belonging to Leighton Hall where, in summer, there are demonstrations of eagles, falcons and various owls in flight. There are one or two footpaths through this rough, wild area but most of it is private and there is now a Clay Pigeon shooting area and a horse riding course.

The Bridleway cuts across the rough limestone country from east to west, terminating at Crag Foot. There is another point marked on the map with the same name. This is half a mile to the north and it is here where there is a telephone box and a conspicuous chimney which, in times past, was used as a pumping station to drain sea water from the flat land ahead; also it once housed a saw mill.

Here there is a footpath which leads through woodland towards the Leighton Hall Estate.

Close to this pathway are spoil heaps from disused mines which produced red ocre for the paint industry. It is advisable to keep away from these for two reasons. Firstly, there are shafts which could collapse. Secondly, the rich red earth could dye your clothes with a pigment which is difficult to remove.

From Crag Foot to the north extends the swampy land of Leighton Moss, skirted by the railway line to Arnside and to the west, we can see the wooded hills around Silverdale, where we are now heading.

Warton to Arnside

8 miles

THIS area is a Mecca for bird-watchers. One mile, towards the north, is Leighton Moss Bird Centre, where the RSPB have made hides from where the bird life on the shallow, reedy water may be observed. Here, on the causeway which divides the two stretches of water, there is a hide open to the public where one may see swans, gulls, herons, coots, all sorts of ducks and field birds. If you are lucky, you may also catch a glimpse of an otter. On a summer evening, the booming cry of the bittern may be heard but you are very fortunate if you can see it among the tall reeds.

The RSPB have converted an old barn into an information centre with car parking facilities, toilets and a cafe.

To the south-west, on the seaward side of the road, there are two more hides open to the public. One of them has been erected as a memorial to Eric Morecambe, the great comedian who was an enthusiastic ornithologist. From here, the route crosses the low lying swampy ground to the wooded headland of Jenny Brown's Point. It is best to avoid high tide if you want to keep your feet dry. Here we have a choice. If the tide is out, we may walk along the sands or scramble over gently sloping sea cliffs following the coastline, past the little beach near Silverdale and north to The Cove. Alternatively, at Jenny Brown's Point, we may decide to proceed along the pleasant lane to Wolf House Gallery, where there is an art and craft centre which also serves excellent coffee and cakes.

The coastline around The Point is interesting. There

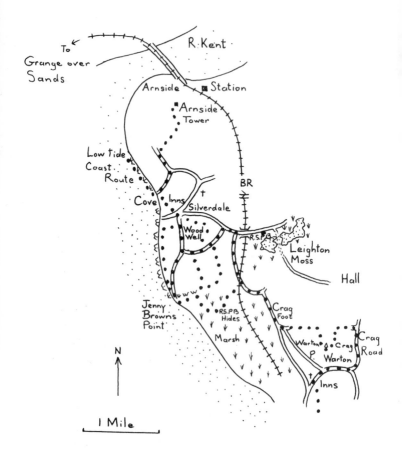

Whitbarrow Scar from Jenny Brown's Point near Silverdale.

stands a prominent chimney which was used for copper smelting and, close by, a breakwater juts into the sea. This was part of an over-ambitious scheme devised to reclaim the land between here and Hest Bank but the company ran into financial difficulties and the project was abandoned. The stone for the construction of this long breakwater was quarried nearby and the flat area below the quarry is now used as a gathering place for sheep.

From Wolf House Gallery, a short walk up the road brings you to a footpath sign on the left, pointing to 'Wood-well'. This leads below a fine limestone escarpment, through the trees to a clearing below. Here is an artificial rectangular pool, formerly a water supply and a watering place for drovers. Behind, under an overhanging rock, there is an ancient trough which is fed by dripping water which has drained below the limestone.

The path to **Silverdale** is marked and passes behind

The Cave, on shore at the cove, Silverdale.

houses into the village. Silverdale, like so many of the villages round the Bay, was once a small cluster of cottages occupied by fishermen. Then, the Victorians developed it as a quiet picturesque retreat. Later, further development took place in the form of modern bungalows, which are now mainly occupied by retired people. Most of the houses have pretty gardens and are discreetly positioned so that, for most of the time, the area retains its atmosphere of unspoiled charm.

There are several pubs, a few shops and a parking area by the seashore. Here, the shallow sea meets the flat turf where sheep graze at low tide. When the tide comes in, however, it does so rapidly and the farmer appears, to herd the sheep to safety. Incidentally, let this be a warning. Don't leave your car on the beach when there is an incoming tide.

Arnside is our next objective and one of the best ways

of getting there is to walk along a path which starts by the roadside about a hundred yards above The Silverdale Hotel. This path goes north-west over meadows for half a mile to The Cove, a delightful little bay surrounded by wooded cliffs and there is an interesting cave situated above a sloping rock face, up which an active person can easily scramble to an entrance. Alas, the cave itself is disappointing, for it only goes in a few yards.

From the Cove our next objective is Hollins Farm and to reach it we walk uphill along the lane passing, on the right, a delightful garden and orchard. This is at its best in springtime when snowdrops, crocus and daffodils are in bloom. At the top of the hill we turn left, following the road for a hundred yards, when a signposted path points to Arnside. Here we may take the path past Arnside Tower and

A little alleyway at Arnside.

hence to The Knott, or strike north-west to Hollins Farm where we join the coastal path.

All the paths in this delightful area are well signposted, and they are so numerous that it is difficult to decide which is the best to follow. The most direct way to The Knott is to go north/north-west to reach the bridle path which skirts The Knott. This is known as Saul's Drive. We reach this at a little crossroads of pathways where a sign indicates that the pathway ahead is not for horses. This is our way and it climbs up a fairly steep, gravelly path to a welcome seat with a splendid view of the bay, with Grange-Over-Sands visible across the water. Nearby is an indicator which points to the various landmarks visible from here, including nearly all the Lakeland peaks.

Continuing uphill, we soon see the strange knotted tree and, behind it, yet another seat and viewpoint.

Fluke fishing , Morecambe Bay. (Taken from picture in Lancaster Maritime Museum)

Arnside

ARNSIDE was originally a port for the mills at Milnthorpe, four miles north-east. It was also a base for fishermen who gathered flukes and cockles from the sands. Horses and carts would wind their way over the glistening wet sands as the tide receded and rake vigorously until the water rose to the surface, bringing with it a harvest of cockles which were boiled, then transported to the market. In addition, flukes, flounders and shrimps are plentiful in the Bay and the trade is still carried on today, although tractors have replaced the horse and cart.

Then, as with other small resorts around the Bay, the Victorians developed Arnside into a quiet holiday resort and a few wealthier people built large houses in the district and made their homes there. All this was made possible by the opening of the Furness Railway which connects Arnside to the main line at Carnforth. In addition, there used to be a railway line from Arnside which ran alongside the Kent Estuary, then crossed the River Bela by a small viaduct on its way north-east. Part of the line is now a public footpath and the stretch from Arnside to Milnthorpe sweeps in a graceful curve by the estuary, where the land meets the sea and the woodland gives way to short sea-washed turf abutting onto the mudflats where waders and seabirds feed.

In addition to its splendid views, this path provides an alternative way of reaching **Milnthorpe**, our next objective.

The construction of the Arnside viaduct meant boats could no longer sail to the port of Milnthorpe and the

The Ship Inn, Sandside, near Arnside.

docks there became obsolete. To compensate for this, a small wharf was constructed at Arnside, close to the railway station. This was eventually destroyed by storms and Arnside was, in turn, abandoned as a port. Recently, a small stone pier has been erected on the site of the old wharf, paid for by public subscription. There it stands, surrounded by gardens and seats from where one may admire the views across the Bay to Grange-Over-Sands, which is surrounded by wooded limestone hills with the Cumbrian mountains beyond. The pier must be one of the smallest in the country but it has a better view than most.

Arnside Knott
(522 feet)

THE area around north Lancashire and southern Cumbria is dotted with limestone hills rising to just over 400 feet: Warton Crag, Whitbarrow Scar, Hutton Roof, Arnside Knott and many others. Below these hills lie quiet villages built from the local stone: Yealand Conyers, Burton, Hutton, Levens, Arnside and Silverdale, to mention just a few. It is a walker's paradise. There are many well marked paths and evidences of wild life and local history.

These hills are miniatures of other, more vast limestone uplands which once lay in horizontal beds, composed of the bones and shells of marine life which existed millions of years ago beneath the seas. Then slowly, the land emerged from the waters and, by the same relentless motion of the earth, it became lifted, folded and tilted. The chemical action of rainwater produced caves and fissures, which are known as grikes, where in a humid atmosphere, protected from the frosts of winter, grow rare plants and ferns. The rocks which rise above the grikes, form limestone pavements known as clints.

A well placed car park is the start for many routes to the summit. On the east side are scree slopes known locally as shilla beds and there are notices asking walkers to avoid them. Efforts are being made to prevent further erosion by putting brushwood reinforcements there and by planting trees.

The railway line from Carnforth to Carlisle curves around the northern side of the area, passing over the

Shetland ponies on Arnside Knott.

River Kent on the viaduct and circling the western coastline of Cumbria close to the mountains of the Lake District. This is surely one of the most scenic lines in the country. At certain times, the 'train buffs' gather, armed with cameras to watch a steam train going over the Kent Viaduct.

It is across these sands that the ancient coach route once ran and there are many stories of past disasters when coaches and their occupants were trapped by the rapid incoming tide. Nowadays the sand crossing should only be carried out under the guidance of Cedric Robinson, 'The Sand Pilot', who at certain times will conduct parties over the sands. It is a memorable trip and those who do it should be prepared to get a soaking perhaps up to the waist, depending upon wind and tide. The original route ran from Hest Bank to Kents bank near

Arnside Tower, an old pele tower.

Grange-over-Sands but now the shorter routes starting from Arnside and Silverdale are preferred.

In 1985, a group of horse-drawn carriages made what may be the last crossing of this kind from Hest Bank to Kents Bank. This historic occasion was organised by The Duke of Edinburgh and supervised by Cedric Robinson.

On the summit of Arnside Knott is a trig. point and a pleasant seat positioned quite close to the skeleton of a strange tree. There used to be more but one by one they have disappeared. The last one is shaped like a huge giraffe and there have been various explanations for its origin. The most romantic is that two lovers entwined the tree saplings together as a symbol of their undying love. Alas, the trees no longer live but around them, new trees are growing and there will always be trees on the top of the Knott. In fact, it is difficult to think of anywhere where there is a more varied selection.

Of all the limestone hills in the area, Arnside Knott is the most popular — and not without reason. The flora and fauna is similar to Warton Crag, with its abundance of wild flowers and variety of woodland but there is an even greater number of paths.

The land to the south-west at Heathwaite is being cleared of some woodland in order to create more sunlight which will encourage plants such as cowslips and which, in turn, attract butterflies to the area. There are several rare species including the Duke of Burgundy Fritillary and also this is one of the few places south of the border where, in summer, the rare Scotch Argus butterfly may be seen. In addition, this area is rich in rock fossils giving evidence that it was, in geological times, covered by the sea. On the south-eat, down among the rich farmland towards Silverdale, lie the ruins of Arnside Tower, one of the best examples of pele towers in the district. There is another good example at Hazelslack, just over a mile north-east. Here, one can easily imagine the local people, along with their cattle gathered behind the safety of the limestone walls which gave protection from the wild Scottish invaders and cattle thieves.

Arnside to Levens

6 miles

FROM the summit of Arnside Knott we walk northwards through woodland until the wall on our left is reached. A stile leads to more open land where larch trees are bent by the wind and brightly coloured fungi grow. Descending the open grassland clipped short by grazing sheep, we head towards a gate in the limestone wall which takes us into the thick woods close to the built up area of Arnside, where one may be tempted to tarry awhile and sample the many cafes, pubs and restaurants or take a walk along the little promenade where we can see wading birds, fishermen and train spotters all busy with their various occupations.

Whichever way we take, our next objective is Fairy Steps, two miles north-east. The path is signposted and we are now on The Limestone Way, which is a thirteen miles link from Arnside to Kirkby Lonsdale. We follow this as far as **Beetham** where our way turns northwards. The pathway starts on the fringe of Arnside on Black Dyke Road where a signpost directs us across the open field to the north-west where we can already see the limestone escarpment of Fairy Steps. With vigilance we cross the railway line from Silverdale and follow the path until, once again, we enter the limestone woodlands as we ascend through rocks to reach the foot of the escarpment. At first sight, this looks like an insurmountable barrier to the walker but a narrow rock staircase brings us onto the flat top of the plateau where larch and pine

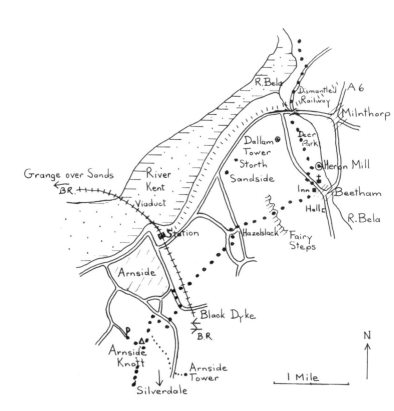

R. Bela

Dismantled Railway   A 6

Milnthorpe

Deer Park

Dallam Tower

Heron Mill

Storth

Sandside

Inn

Beetham

Grange over Sands

BR.

River Kent

Viaduct

Hall

R. Bela

Station

Hazelslack

Fairy Steps

Arnside

Black Dyke

B.R.

P

Arnside Knott

N

Arnside Tower

1 Mile

Silverdale

66

The Fairy Steps near Beetham.

trees grow and from where we are rewarded with yet another breathtaking view.

Now the path descends towards the delightful village of Beetham. It is delightful for the lovely limestone cottages with their flower-filled gardens, for the carpets of snowdrops in springtime, for the old limestone church opposite 'The Wheatsheaf Hotel'.

From here, follow the lane north-west for a hundred yards, then turn right down a little pathway which leads to Heron Mill. This is an old water mill which has been renovated into full working order and is open to the public. The River Bela provides the source of power whilst, on the other side of the river, accessible by a new wooden bridge, is a modern paper mill.

The weir which provides the head of water for Heron Mill is part of a natural limestone wall and there is a tiny

Snowdrops in the woods, near Beetham.

underground passage leading through it which may tempt those who don't mind getting wet feet. The River Bela is a beautiful river and it is worthwhile lingering in this pleasant spot where one may catch a glimpse of a heron, kingfisher or dipper.

Just opposite the Heron Mill is a stile which leads us into an entirely different landscape, the parkland of Dallam Tower. The scene is reminiscent of that from a south country mansion with the tranquil river winding its way round the grassy knoll where a herd of fallow deer graze. The house is occupied by the Wilson family and was built in 1720. The path climbs the hill then descends to the road near to the bridge, a quarter of a mile to the west of Milnthorpe.

Immediately to the right of the bridge, a little lane follows the river, passing close to where once the old rail-

Heron Mill, Beetham. An old waterwheel cornmill which has been restored to working condition and is open to the public.

Pele Tower at Beetham, nearto the A6 road, halfway between Lancaster and Kendal. It stands next to a farm and is not open to the public, although a pathway runs nearby.

way line from Arnside crossed the River Bela by an aqueduct. On the left a stile leads to a footpath which follows the River Kent towards Levens Hall. This is not marked as a right of way, yet is commonly used by locals as a pleasant stroll amid tranquil surroundings. We may follow the path beside an embankment, walking on soft sea-washed turf dotted with sea pinks. Care should be taken to avoid this section at high tides. The river may be followed as far as Ninezergh Farm when a lane leads us to the right, bringing the walker to the A6 road close to Levens Hall.

If the walker has doubts about this section, there is an obvious alternative in following the lane across flat farmland, then turning right to emerge onto the A6 at either

The River Bela, near Milnethorpe. The road to Arnside goes over the bridge.

The Blue Bell Hotel, or a mile further north near to Levens Bridge.

Incidentally, in the little village of Heversham, just on the opposite side of the A6, is another fine limestone church. In the porch is a good example of a Viking Cross with evidence of dual allegiance to Christianity and to the old pagan gods. From here, there are footpaths leading north which pass Leasgill to bring us onto the A6 near to Levens Bridge. It is worth noting that Levens Bridge does not go over the River Levens, but over the Kent.

Levens Hall

LIKE many other mansions in the area, Levens was originally a pele tower. The original building was erected about 1250 by the de Redman family. It was, like Arnside Tower, a square, gaunt building. In the sixteenth century it passed to James Bellingham (cousin of the de Redmans). He enlarged the place, converted it into a comfortable residence and furnished it accordingly. Alas, his great grandson, Alan, lost the entire estate by gambling and it was sold to his kinsman, Colonel James Grahme, who further enlarged and enhanced it.

The present owner, Hal Bagot, is related to the Grahme family and took residence just after the Second World War, when the Hall had been

neglected for some time. He set about restoring the buildings and adding exquisite furnishings which are now there to be admired by the public who come to visit the Hall. Apart from the fine displays of furnishings, tapestry, pictures and pottery inside the Hall, there are fine gardens with extensive topiary work and a small but interesting collection of steam engines.

Levens to Brigsteer

4 miles

ACROSS the busy A6 road is the entrance to the parkland which has two footpaths, one on each side of the River Kent. They climb gently up the hill where there is a herd of Norwegian black fallow deer and also a herd of unusual Bagot goats. There are also some splendid trees, including some magnificent American Redwoods, an avenue of ancient oaks and some fine chestnuts.

The path ascends towards the A59 clearway which is avoided first by a most unique pathway underneath. Fur-

Leven's Park. There are two public footpaths crossing this park which is carefully tended by the Bagot family at Levens. There are splendid oak and chestnut trees surrounding the River Kent.

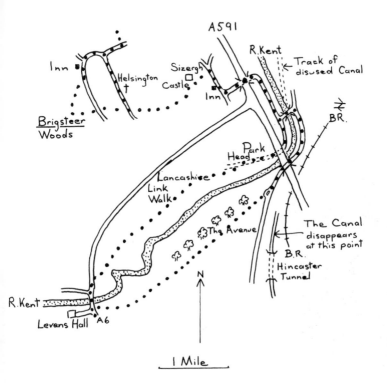

Brigsteer Woods. Carpeted by wild Daffodils in springtime, owned by the National Trust and traversed by beautiful pathways.

ther on a small road tunnel leads to the old A6, conveniently handy for the Strickland Arms pub.

At Park Head, the River Kent rushes below the road in a series of cataracts and waterfalls where in early November, the salmon may be seen leaping over rocks as they try to reach their spawning grounds upstream. There is a fine riverside path from here to Kendal but our route climbs gently westwards to the limestone hills.

So far, our route has been easy to follow but here, close to Park Head, we have a complexity of river, roads and bridges, so that a detailed diagram may help the walker to find a safe way towards Sizergh Castle, our next objective.

Sizergh Castle

The pub at Sizergh is called 'The Strickland Arms', and for a very good reason: the nearby castle has been occupied by the Strickland family since the thirteenth century. Throughout these years, they have been knights of the shires, members of parliament and they have fought in many battles, including Agincourt when Sir Thomas carried the banner of St George. The descendants of the family still occupy part of the castle, which is now owned by the National Trust and is open to the public from April to October. Inside, there are fine collections of pictures, furniture, panelling and a splendid Elizabethan fireplace.

Perhaps the most memorable aspects of the castle are the gardens. To the west is a small lake set

amidst magnificent rockery, whilst on the opposite side of the buildings is a large ornamental lake surrounded by exotic flowering plants and trees. To complete the picture, the swans glide gracefully over the waters which reflect the towering ramparts of the castle.

Like so many castles in the area, it was once a pele tower which over the years has been enlarged into a fine Elizabethan mansion. It is approached by a narrow road which passes through parkland leading to the south side of the buildings where there is the public entrance. This road curves round to the westerly side of the estate and it is there that our way continues. If the woods at Brigsteer are our choice of route, follow the left hand cart track which runs in a south-westerly direction. The alternative is to cross the fields making north-west to Holeslack Farm where we join the lane which climbs up to the little church at Helsington.

Brigsteer to Burneside
5^1/2 miles

From Helsington Church, there is yet another choice. Ahead lies the unfenced lane which leads to the road from Brigsteer to Kendal, whilst below are the woodlands of Brigsteer. If it is springtime, then there is only one answer, that is to descend to the wood where there is "a host of golden daffodils, nodding and dancing in the breeze". Wordsworth was not writing about Brigsteer but I am quite sure that he would have been at least equally inspired. Not only daffodils but violets and primroses and, if we are quiet, perhaps a glimpse of deer or a squirrel.

It's only a short walk but in springtime it is a walk through paradise. When the stile at the edge of the woods is reached, the field ahead is crossed to where the narrow road may be followed past a white-washed cottage with a most delightful garden, then on to the village of **Brigsteer**, almost resembling an alpine hamlet as it nestles below the steep wooded hillside, but with the added advantage of a pub at the crossroads! From here, ascend the road on the right which soon brings you, once again, to the limestone escarpment leading across Helsington Barrows. As we walk along the high limestone ridge, we pass some fine larches, bent by the wind and in May and June there is a profusion of wild orchids.

The elevated path takes us north to a strange circular shelter upon the summit. On the under side of the roof is a fine topographical diagram which indicates all the high points which may be seen from here. Now, alas, it is

BRIGSTEER TO BURNESIDE 5¼ MILES

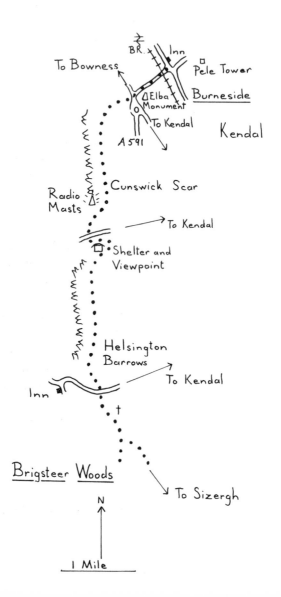

To Bowness

BR.

Inn

Pele Tower

Burneside

△ Elba Monument

To Kendal

A 591

Kendal

Cunswick Scar

Radio Masts △

To Kendal

Shelter and Viewpoint

Helsington Barrows

To Kendal

Inn

†

Brigsteer Woods

To Sizergh

N

1 Mile

been defaced by idiots! However, nothing can spoil the view from here. From the starting place for our walk in the flat lands of the Fylde in the hazy south, to the northern hills of Lakeland which now beckon us.

So, we now descend to the Kendal road which is crossed. There is a small car park and, on the far side, some radio masts which serve as a landmark, if such were needed. Beyond lies Cunswick Scar, which is really a continuation of the limestone ridge. This is wide, open land, decked with blue moorland grass. Below us to the west, are rocky paths leading through woodland towards a secluded tarn but we ignore these and continue along the watershed until reaching a stile which leads to a pleasant descending path. This brings us to a minor road, then on over farmland towards the busy A591 Windermere road which we cross with great care. The prominent stone column ahead is called The Elba monument erected to mark the end of the Napoleonic Wars. This is a useful landmark to point our direction to the little winding lane which leads down to **Burneside** where the railway level crossing is passed. This is the Oxenholme to Windermere line. Half a mile beyond the village is yet another pele tower which is now the working farm at Burneside Hall.

This is the point where we link to The Dales Way which goes from Windermere to Ilkley. This, in turn, joins the Coast to Coast path from West Cumberland to Robin Hood's Bay in Yorkshire. It would be quite possible to continue along this delightful walk as far as Keld and join The Pennine Way. This presents many intriguing possi-

Strickland Arms, Sizergh. Now bypassed by the A591 clearway, under which, the old road is conveyed by a tunnel leading to Leven's Park.

Extinct canal near Kendal. This is not on our route, but it is a pleasant, shorter alternative way of reaching Kendal.

The Lakeland mountains from the hills above Kendal. From left to right we can see the Coniston mountains, Crinkle Crags, Bowfell and the Langdale Pikes.

Helsington Barrows, south of Kendal. A fine pathway crosses the Limestone escarpment in the picture.

Burneside.

Burneside pele tower, 2 miles north of Kendal. Here our route joins the Dales Way which links to the Pennine Way and the Coast to Coast route.

bilities of, for instance, finishing our walk at Edale, or Kirk Yetholme in Scotland or on the Yorkshire Coast.

For the more modest walker, however, the route continues alongside the River Kent which is joined on the northern end of Burneside.

Kendal

KATHERINE PARR was the last wife of Henry VIII and she is famous for being the only one to survive that monarch. She was born at Kendal Castle, which was built in the twelfth century by a Norman knight, Gilbert Fitz Reinfred. The castle eventually passed to Sir Thomas de Parr who was Master of the Wards and Comptroller to the King. So, although it is likely that his daughter spent her early life in Kendal, she lived at court or perhaps at one of their estates in the south of England. The ruins of the castle stand prominently on the hill to the east of the town.

The motto of Kendal is 'Wool is my bread'. This refers to the original trade of the town, built upon the woollen industry derived from the tough Herdwick sheep which graze on the mountains of Cumbria. They are tough too, as is their wool and the mutton. The shepherds who tend the sheep are also tough but both sheep and shepherds have to withstand the climate of the mountains - especially in winter when sheep are frequently buried in snowdrifts and the shepherd and his dog climb up into Arctic conditions to rescue them. Looking down from the castle, the River Kent can be seen. It flows past Abbot Hall which houses a museum of Lakeland life and industry, and then passes the 'K' boot and shoe factory. This was founded by the Somervell family. The most famous of this local family was Doctor Howard Somervell who was on the 1924 Everest expedition and was one of the last persons to see Mallory and Irvine alive, before they disappeared into the mists of Everest. Did they reach the summit? The question will probably never

Kendal Castle, on the hilltop east of the town. A good view-point of the Cumbrian mountains to the north-east.

be answered but many climbers, like myself, would like to think that they were the first.

Kendal also provided an essential item for those early expeditions — Kendal Mint Cake. There are several references to it in the early records of the pre-war accounts, which relate how the climbers paused to take a bite of their mint cake and, feeling much better, continued their struggle up the mountain.

Another notable Kendal character was Alfred Wainwright, who was born in south Lancashire but spent much of his life in Kendal, working in the treasurer's office until retirement when he devoted his life to the production of the mountain guides which have made him famous.

Kendal is 'the gateway to the Lake District' and it is to there that we are heading, so open the gate and let's continue our walk northwards - on towards Staveley and Windermere.

Burneside to Windermere

9 miles

IT is only three miles from Burneside to Staveley and the Kent is followed, along The Dales Way.

The River Kent is reputed to be one of the fastest flowing rivers in England. It is only just over twenty miles long and descends from the slopes of High Street, 2,700 feet above sea level, down to Morecambe Bay. It provided water power for numerous mills on its turbulent way - bobbin mills at Staveley, snuff mills at Helsington and paper mills at Bowston and Kendal. Many of these industries exist no longer and those surviving, mainly now use other means of power but the sheer number of mills suggests that there must have been quite a large working population. Indeed, in the nineteenth century, there was a bigger ratio of industrial working population in this part of Cumbria than in Birmingham.

At **Bowston,** the quiet road is crossed by walking a few yards to the right, then picking up the riverside path which leads into **Staveley,** which has regained its tranquillity, being recently bypassed by the busy A591 road to Windermere.

In contrast, our way follows lanes marked as cul-de-sacs so it is rarely that a car is seen disturbing the peace of this quiet corner of Lakeland. Yes, we are now in The Lake District National Park and our journey from Lancashire is nearly completed.

Our lane runs parallel to the Kent but as it climbs, the

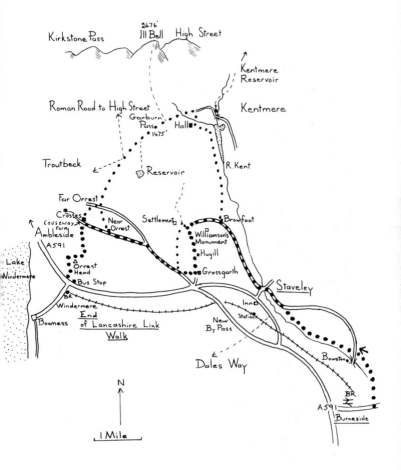

Kirkstone Pass

2476'
Ill Bell   High Street

Kentmere
Reservoir

Roman Road to High Street

Kentmere

Garburn
Pass
1475'
Hall

Troutbeck

Reservoir

R. Kent

Far Orrest

Crosses
Causeway
farm
Ambleside
A591

Near
Orrest

Settlement

Brownfoot

Williamson's
Monument

Hugill

Lake
Windermere

Orrest
Head

Bus Stop

Grossgarth

Staveley

BR
Windermere
End
of Lancashire Link
Walk

Bowness

Inn

Station

New
By Pass

Dales Way

Bowstone

BR

N

A591
Burneside

1 Mile

river is left below as Browfoot Farm is passed and the road soon terminates at a 'T' junction where it joins the bridleway from Kentmere to Ings.

When the bridleway is joined, we follow the southern track but, if time permits and the walker is interested in pre-history, it is well worth while diverting along the northern way for a mile to have a look at the settlement above Borrans Tarn. Piles of stones, foundations of buildings are scattered over an acre of land in a shallow basin, sheltered and secluded. There is not a lot to see, yet anyone with interest and imagination can visualise this community which lived there thousands of years ago. There are many more in the area and it is difficult to ascertain the dates of the early settlements. One authority even says that their age could be anything between two to four thousand years.

The number of these known settlements indicates that there must have been quite a large population and we know that in Neolithic times there was a thriving industry engaged in the making and exporting of axe heads. The main centre was high up on Pike O'Stickle in the Langdale Pikes and there are many more. Examples of Langdale axes have been found all over Britain and even abroad. The people who made the axes did not live in the inhospitable surroundings high in the mountains but went there during the summer months. So it is quite probable that they chose to live in places such as these settlements where the land was fertile and the climate less severe. No one knows for certain. They could have been occupied much later, by the iron age people or even during the Roman occupation when they would live in security and safety.

Returning to our main route, the bridleway towards Ings is followed, passing below a prominent cairn upon the hill to the left. This is Williamson Monument (901 feet). On it is the inscription, "In memory of Thomas Williamson of Height in Hugil, Gent, who died Feb 13th 1797 Aged 66 years. Erected 1803". Heights is the next farm on our journey and Thomas Williamson used to climb up to this spot every morning before breakfast. There is no pathway but it can be reached by going through an iron gate then, with some difficulty (for larger folk), threading the little snick in the corner of the wall and finding a pleasant grassy walk to the summit, which commands splendid views from the hills around Windermere to the Kentmere Valley, with High Street in the distance.

Our bridleway continues past The Heights Farm, after which a footpath on the right leads to Grassgarth, St Anns and Broadgate Farms, where the metalled road is taken for a mile and after passing Near Orrest Farm, the footpath up to Orrest Head rises on the left. The area round us is hilly, quiet farming land. It is in close proximity to the busy tourist routes to central Lake District yet it retains its tranquillity.

Since leaving the Kendal area, we have passed out of the limestone country into a landscape made of even older rocks which were laid as the mud deposits of shallow seas. Further north, in central Lakeland the rocks are volcanic. These form some of the highest mountains of Cumbria and they are a delight to the rock climbers because of the firmness and hardness of the rock.

Millions of years ago, the limestone rocks completely covered Lakeland and they rose to a height comparable

A very simplified geology of the Lake District.

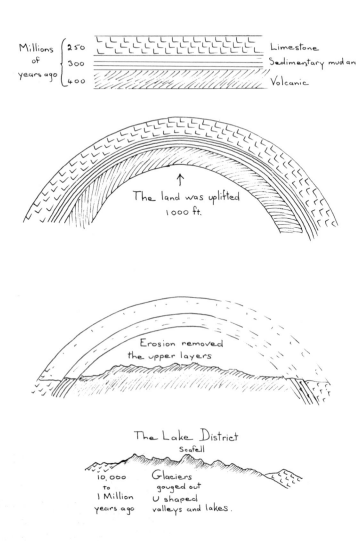

Millions of years ago
- 250 — Limestone
- 300 — Sedimentary mud an[d]
- 400 — Volcanic

The land was uplifted 1000 ft.

Erosion removed the upper layers

The Lake District

Scafell

10,000 to 1 Million years ago

Glaciers gouged out U shaped valleys and lakes.

with The Himalayas. Erosion has worn away the topmost layers, leaving the volcanic rocks of central Lakeland sur-rounded by limestone hills and the gentle Silurian land-scape, through which we are now passing, as we approach the final stage of our walk to Orrest Head, above Windermere.

Many people consider that the finest mountain views are not gained from the highest peaks but often from quite modest hilltops. Orrest Head is a typical example of this and the panorama extends from Morecambe Bay to the high peaks of The Scafell range. Below us, Winder-mere stretches from the low hills around Newby Bridge to Ambleside, which is at the heart of the climbing country. The Langdale Pikes are prominent, as is Conis-ton Old Man and Helvellyn.

So, our walk finishes here on a high note, with one of

Orrest Head, above Windermere. Kentmere Valley is below and, in the distance are the mountains around High Street.

The Roman road, High Street. This road started at Ravensglass on the Cumbrian coast and went through Ambleside to cross the mountains northwards towards Penrith. It passes our route near to Troutbeck.

the best views in the District. All that now remains is to saunter down the pathway which becomes a wooded lane leading right into Windermere where there is a bus stop and railway station handy to take us home again.

For those who may have sufficient time there is a final variation to our walk which is possible. This involves continuing up Kentmere along the western side of the narrow Kentmere Tarn, then following the ancient bridleway south-west over Garburn Pass. This will put an extra six miles onto the route, making the total distance from Staveley to Windermere, thirteen miles.

Anyone choosing this route will find it very rewarding as it skirts round some of the less frequented eastern fells of the Lake District. In fact, the close proximity of Ill Bell

Windermere Lake from Orrest Head.

must be a temptation for those who still have sufficient energy to climb this fine rocky peak, which we have seen so often as we travelled northwards. When reaching the junction on the descent of Garburn Pass, take the second left towards Far Orrest.

By this time, we must be ready for the fleshpots of Windermere or there may be a train in the station waiting to take us back to our starting point in Lancashire. Windermere was until recently the boundary of Westmorland and the Furness part of Lancashire and there are many in that area, which is now Cumbria, who still consider themselves to be Lancastrians. Be that as it may, our walk has linked rural Lancashire to the lakes and mountains of Cumbria.

"Crossing Lancaster Sands"

J. M. W. Turner
(1775-1851)

Courtesy Birmingham Museum and Art Gallery

To celebrate Lancaster's close association with the Lake District, Turner's sublime painting has been reproduced as a folding fine quality art card by Lancaster Tourism. The card is supplied wrapped in cellophane and is suitable for use as a distinctive greetings card, or for framing. To obtain your copy please send just two First Class stamps to the address below. You will also recieve a free Lancaster Visitors' Pack, with further information of Lancaster's many historic and scenic attractions. If you require the Visitors' Pack without the card, simply write, phone or fax.

> **'The Lancashire-Lakeland Link Offer',**
> **Lancaster Tourism,**
> **29 Castle Hill,**
> **Lancaster LA1 1YN.**
> **Tel: (0524) 32878**
> **Fax: (0524) 847472**